# When Sheeps Weep

# When Sheeps Weep

*Where Eagles Fly*

Akeam Simmons

*iUniverse books may be ordered through booksellers or by contacting:*

*iUniverse*
*1663 Liberty Drive*
*Bloomington, IN 47403*
*www.iuniverse.com*
*1-800-Authors (1-800-288-4677)*



*ISBN: 978-1-5320-1969-2 (sc)*
*ISBN: 978-1-5320-1970-8 (e)*

*Print information available on the last page.*

*iUniverse rev. date: 03/09/2017*

# Contents

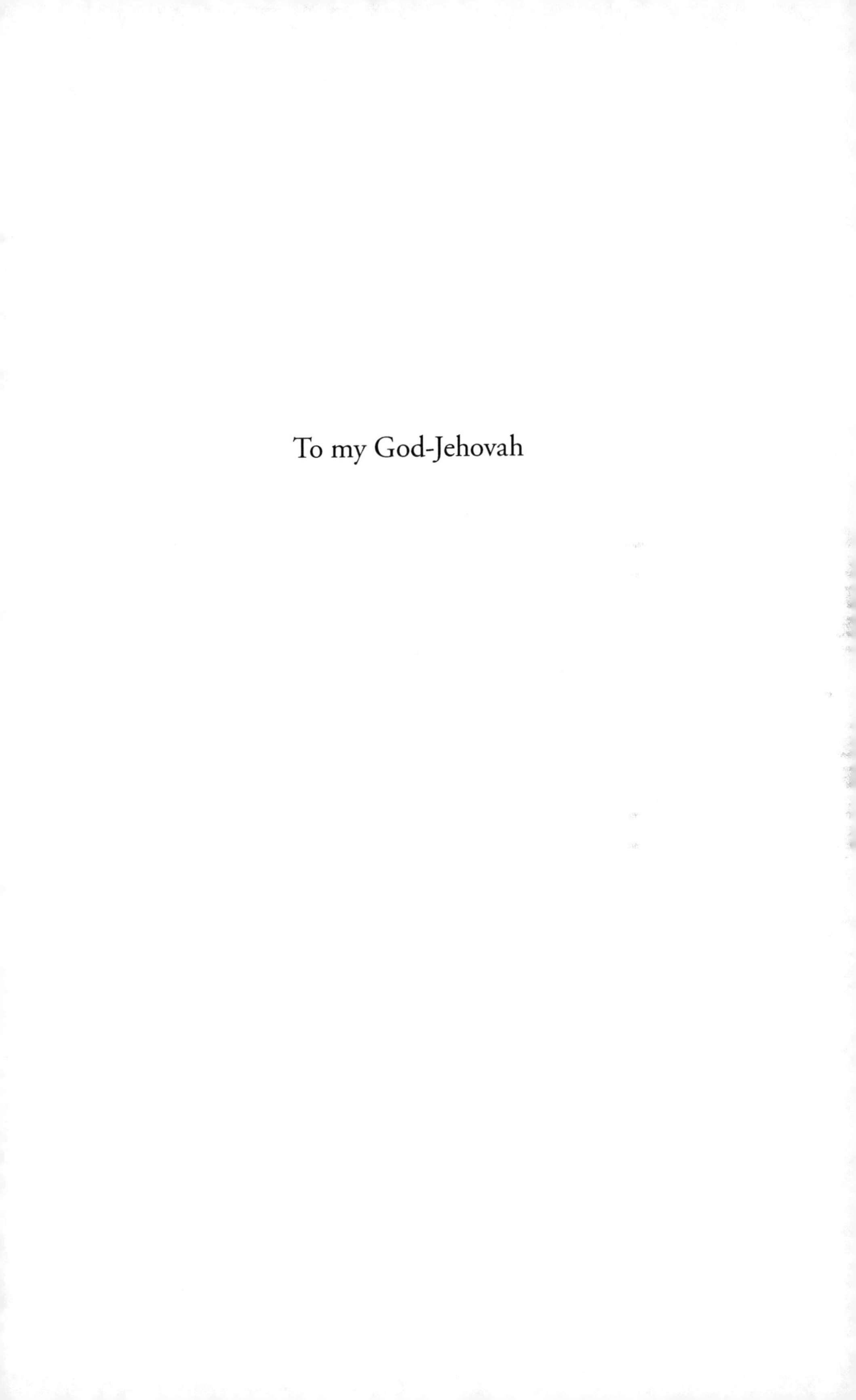

To my God-Jehovah

# PROVERBS

-Never show your hand
Until you are beginning to play your hand
Else you give those to which you play against
Time to adjust for your attack

-It is the one that dips in the cup with you
That indeed does you most harm
For he is the one you least expect

-Failure is but another opportunity
To succeed

-Watch the one that whispers in your ear
For often poison flows from their lips

-Choose to live, and you will live to choose

# I SAW GOD YESTERDAY

I saw God yesterday
Though He was not in a church

I saw God yesterday
Though He was not on the mountain

I saw God yesterday
Though He was not riding the sea

I saw God yesterday
Though He was not on Capital Hill

I saw God yesterday
Though He walked not amongst the kings and presidents

I saw God yesterday
Though He was not amongst the preachers

I saw God yesterday
Though He was not heading a religious assembly

I saw God yesterday
In a small corner of an isolated street
A street that man had long forgotten
Nestled among wrinkled News Papers of no news

I saw God yesterday
Glaring back at me with eyes so pure
From an orphanage filled with innocence
And hope and love unfeigned

I saw God yesterday
Walking the sinful pavement of city streets
Hoping someone would see Him
And invite Him in

I saw God yesterday
Outside of the marble church
With pretty stained glass windows
Hoping for somebody to pray

I saw God yesterday
Going into a shack where Christmas had long forgotten
But love was heaping abundance

I saw God yesterday
Sitting and laughing upon Skid Row
Of better tomorrows and temporary sorrows
With souls that time had simply burrowed
And tossed on the road with no plans to follow

I saw God yesterday
And I brought Him home with me
And asked Him to use me to be
The light for others to see
The God that is inside of me
As deep as the ragging sea
But shallow enough for the failing eyes to see
The conditions and situations that would not let me be free
The wrinkled news-less News Papers He looked passed to see me

I Saw God Yesterday
He filled my today with enough splendors for tomorrow
And enough hope to get rid of my earthly sorrow

# LETTER FROM MAMA

I saw you yesterday pretending at my funeral
Yelling and crying over my casket
When you wouldn't even come visit me when I was sick
And wouldn't talk to me when I was lonely

Why are you crying now
I hurt no more
I am lonely no more
My tears have been wiped away

I know that you don't weep for me
Your tears are for those around you
Who feel sorrow for what you pretend to go through
Hush before I weep over here where there is no weeping

But I fooled you
For you knew not that I left a will
A will that is sure to bring you real tears
And bitter bills

Oh you don't miss me now
But you will
When there is no one else to turn to
And nobody else cares of what you're going through

But even now I still love you
Even amidst your fake tears and hollowed sobs
Would that I could turn love off
But mama always loves her child

**That's how God made us**
**To love you in-spite of your faults**
**Regardless of the way that you treated me**
**Even on the other side of the grave**
**My love for my child still lingers on**
**If I could come back**
**I would**
**And put my arms around you**
**Even when I know you don't really care about me**

**All of my stuff that you wanted so badly**
**Take it**
**for soon you will need it**
**I forgive you for abandoning me**
**When I needed you the most**

**And though I can't come to you**
**For now there is a gulf separating me and you**
**I still watch over you**
**And hope that someday your heart will soften too**
**And your eyes will open anew**

**Now I close my letter**
**But never my love**
**Until we meet upon the peaceful shores**
**Love mama**

# OH SOUL OF MAN

Oh how wretched am I
That weeps and cry
Who fail to bid good bye
To things that causes me to die

Oh soul of man

I be but an earthen vessel
Overcome by things to wrestle
Living every day to hustle
With things beyond mere muscle

Oh soul of man

Hopelessly I die a little every day
Still not yet learning how to pray
Or what things to the master I should say
Of the mortal sins I must pay
Oh soul of man

Another struggle another breath
Worried about good health
And worldly wealth
Of how I should contain before my appointed death

Oh soul of man

Eat drink and be merry for tomorrow we but die
And amongst our forefathers we will lie
In-spite of the tears we do cry
Still we must die
And bid the world farewell and goodbye

**Oh soul of man**

**A many a battles I have fought**
**Some small some great but many a lessons I was taught**
**Right down to how to achieve the many a things I sought**
**Oh soul of man**

**So now I** shall **not seek to rest**
**While on life's rout to fulfill my test**
**To weaned and glean the best**
**Before journeying to my eternal rest**

**Oh soul of man**

# MY DADDY'S EYES

I Look in the mirror and I see
My daddy's eyes staring back at me
Oh how can this be
When yesterday he refused to raise me
And teach me what a man I should be

My daddy's eyes

I don't see how
He could stare back at me now
When over the years he refused me even the milk of a cow

My daddy's eyes

But there he is looking back at me
Smiling a little can't you see
Proud of what he sees in me
Of what mama alone reared me to be

My daddy's eyes

To my high school graduation
He had no invitation
Because he wasn't there helping during my struggling situations
Helping mama protect me from the world's annihilation

My daddy's eyes

How dare he show up in my mirror
Secretly beckoning to become dearer
While death eases upon him ever so nearer
But there he is staring back at me in my mirror

My daddy's eyes

Forgiveness he screams out to me silently
I scream back amongst shattered glass now I am free
And mama has long gone home peaceably
Only after raising me to be the man that I should be

My daddy's eyes

I look down upon the floor at the broken glass
And I still see through one of the pieces his cast
Staring back at me with tears over the years he has mask
I pick up a piece and I see tears flowing down my daddy's face
Knowing full well of all the pain he can't erase

My daddy's eyes

But to be the man that I should be
I have got to forgive him for failing to be the man he should be
I forgive you daddy for forsaking mama and me
And thanks for looking in on me
Even if it was only through the mirror that I could see
The pain filled eyes begging forgiveness from me

My daddy's eyes

# A MESS

What a mess
What a mess
I have just made a mess
Being so impatient, so impulsive, just a mess
Over filling my days and nights with prolonged stress

I leaped when I should have watched and pray
And not been overly concerned about what people say
Now I sit in folly trying desperately to chase my troubles away
And keep these plaguing demons at bay

Oh how must I achieve my best
Or walk in being bless
When I have just made a mess a terrible mess
And how to come out of this I can only guess

But I will come out of this situation
And next time have much reservation
Before I jump into something without premeditation
And never again cause myself this much degradation
Through undisclosed lethal unwarranted manipulation

# My Race

Oh howling wind oh scorching sun
Flee from me till work is done
And reap of life till I have some
And run this race till I have won

I spend my strength till I have none
Then the world will know where I am from
And help me through this race to run
Till my eyes close and my father's mercy be spun

# Secrets

Oh save me early morning from last night's night
And drive away those secret demons from which I fight
Shoo them back you early morning light
So my righteousness may shine ever so bright

Let the darkness fall away
And make my secrets go astray
Till my nights turn blissfully gay
Where my stars shine during my day

Hide beyond the mountains you glimmering moon
For the light is coming soon
To completely blot out my sin of secrets before noon
Dispelling my nervous unveiling doom

My secrets
Oh God my secrets
Pulling at me piercing me through with yesterday's debts
And lost hollowed unholy bets
Of which I daily fret

Oh that my soul would hide within the light
Like everybody else I'll act like I am alright
And fight and fight
Till my secret no longer taunts me day and night

But secrets they are
Haunting me taunting me of things near and far
Trying to put out my shining star

But I will bring my own secrets to the light
Then take away their power and might
Of me trying to hide my unholy fight
Trying to keep my secrets secret while walking right

Oh here here they are my secrets of me
For all to see
Now oh now I am free from the weight of secrecy

# BLACK ME

My skin is black because the sun rested upon my fathers
And cleaved to my mothers
My blackness pushes justice farther
And causes love among my colorless brothers to falter

My God took the clay from the earth and colored me
He curled my hair and smoothed my skin gallantly
That I might be free
To race with the sun shining on me

And though injustice reign because of the color of my skin
They cannot erase that my father is first from whence God begin
Many a things come and go but my blackness is not a trend
Though sometimes it's mixed with others and forced to blend
Still I am black through and through from start to end

God took the best of Him and made the best of me
So if you look past my color and see me
You'll see God's best on display in me
And all of His marvelous wonders for all to see

From mother earth I was born
From my father's land I was torn
To the slave masters I was joined
And cruelty of my situation caused me to mourn

Oh but my masters couldn't steal my pride
And my royalty they could not hide
For all the cruelty they threw at me I took in stride
Because constantly to the God of heaven I confide

Daily they try to make me forget my past
But my future shoots forth from my past
And the king in me enables me to stand fast
Breaking away the image of me that they try to cast

My color is not a curse
Even though over the years this they tried to nurse
Trying to make me feel my color is a curse
But I am the seed of royalty because God made me first

So now I'll lift my head up and walk proudly
Shouting to the world of whose I am out loudly
Because my God took the best of Him and made the best of me

# OVER YOU

You never told me that we were through
You never told me that you had moved on
Never told me that you were done
And never gave me the kiss of goodbye

Now I remind my heart that we are over you
I remind my tears to cease to flow
And remind my flesh to hush and scream your name no more
I am over you

Hush oh beating heart
Flee oh rolling tears
For my feet must forge down new paths
And my arms must be lonely no more

Yesterday is past and gone
My today is filled with hopes of tomorrow
Of new discoveries
Of new love to forget yesterday's sorrow

Now I laugh for my heart mourns no more
Now I laugh for weeping only endures for a moment
Now I laugh for joy comes after the tears of sorrow

I have to jar myself and remind myself of yesterday's you
Casue I am so over you

# SOMETHING ABOUT THAT GIRL

Something about the way you walk
Something about the way you talk
Something about the way you caught
Something about me you effortlessly bought

Something about the way you flow
Something about the way you glow
Something about even the places you go
Something about where you grow

You I want to know
From your head right down to your pretty little toe
You affect how my winds blow
And secretly feel like another John Doe

In your life I will sow
Because I know not how to utter no
Sailing away from life's belligerent woe
Down joy filled paths we shall go

On and on I go
Riding upon winds that only God blow
Freely riding like the ravenous crow
Pulled by desire that only I know

I fight and fight this holy tow
Of things too deep for me to row
How beauty and splendor can rest on someone I want to know
To bath me in such a lovely glow
So my heart leaps and bellow
For you I've covet to follow
That I may rest from life toils and wrestle no more
For your heart now belongs to me the joyful fellow

# PROVERBS

-The children's personality will not stray far from their parents

-Loyalty among subjects is priceless

-He that cannot keep your secrets or uncovers your weaknesses
Is not your friend

-A fool can be easily fooled
Because he is but a fool

-Money uncovers the true nature of all men

-One will never have enough money to buy character

-Faithfulness is measured by secrecy

-A woman will never be more than she has already been

-It does not matter how well you dress a hog
He will always be but a hog

-The place always image its inhabitants
To change the place, you must first change the man in the place

-A woman will never tell on herself
But her eyes refuse to keep secrets

-When all else fail, pray
When all else succeed, pray
Never eat from your enemy's table
For it reaps of death for you

Do not party with your enemy
Else you become the party

The mouth of a fool will always declare that
He is but a fool

To maintain power, the best a leader can be to his subordinates is cordial, For friendship and anything else breads insolence

# Yesterday's tears

Oh God Oh God when will yesterday leave me alone
And allow peace back in my mortal home
My tears my sorrows constantly drawn
From a well buried deep down in my fragile bones

Secretly silently of you I weep
And my broken heart won't let me sleep
My counselor beg of me to just let you rest and be
But the little child in me won't allow me to be free

You left me
You chose to leave me
I wanted you to fight on so badly
But I know that you were tired and wanted to be free
Of the sickness and disease that bruised you constantly

I don't rightly know why I can't move on
Every time I think I am alright, memories of you I am shown
My heart and mind have just been blown
By immeasurable grief all men will someday be shown

I stand at your grave and talk to you softly
Hoping that you will talk back to me
But from this world you are free
So there is a gulf hindering you from talking back to me

Oh that I might have one more time to say goodbye
But you already know that I would want one more time of goodbye
And one more time of goodbye
And one more time of goodbye

I look in the mirror and I see you looking back at me
Reminding me that you haven't fully left me
I still hear your voice calling out to me
Instructing me
Of what I should be

And when I act out of character I hear you scolding me straighten up
No you hadn't fully left me; I still feel you in my daily cup
When life's situations badly erupt
Imagines of you interrupt
And reminds me I am still your little pup

So sleep on and take your rest
For you have fulfilled your earthly test
Now lay your head in the master's chest
And sleep the sleep that he awards the best
Until I come at last to join you in my own immortal rest

# IN ME

-I watch and guard against my enemy
And protect myself from where he will be
Then I realize that my real enemy
Is locked up inside of me

-Oh you can't see my real enemy
For he hides deep inside of me
Quenching the things that I should be
And trying hard to disrupt my destiny

-In me resides royalty
Between faithfulness and specialty
Gallops my reality
Of things of hopes that I should be

-In me in my bosom rests kings
Alluring queens to come to honor and sing
Of the holy of holies signature ring
On things so utterly wonderful to cling

-In me I see what some refuse to see
The greater part of me
A resting giant waiting to be
The uniqueness of just being me

-The prisons built by me for me
Cannot hold the real me
Who sores the skies ever so glee
And pays the price to be continuously free

OPEN REBUKE

IS BETTER THAN PRIVATE SCOLDING

OR SECRET SCORN

# PROVERBS

-It is most difficult to convince a slave that he is free
And just as difficult to convince a free man to be a slave
For the slave never sees himself more than a slave
And the free man never sees himself less than free

-My face hardly shows what I've been through

-My tears wash my soul of things too toxic for me to carry

-You will never be more than what you already think you are
And you will never be less than what you've accepted yourself to be

-The only power that your enemy has over you
Is the power that you give to him

-Be true to yourself
For no one is better at being you than you

-Better to walk alone
Than walk with someone that means you no good

-If you listen very carefully and don't interrupt
Men will unveil the secrets of their hearts

-It is easy to deceive a man of vanity

-Only a fool utters his whole heart
Some things are best left in the secret chambers of your bosom

-Never follow a blind man
For he will lead you to a place that you don't want to go
-Only a fool will run into where angels fear to go

-unveiling your secrets strips the talebearer of his power

-Only a fool will be insubordinate to the king, for the king will always remember when the fool disrespected him as king, and opportunity will always present itself for the king to chastise the fool

-Though the king forgives right now for the sake of the kingdom, he will always remember your insults, and sooner than later, punish you for them

-Friends are like waves of the sea. They first come in roaring, but soon fizzle out and then leave you

-An ambitious man's motives are never pure

-There is nothing that is entirely free; all things come with a price

-There is great strength in the tears that a man sheds

-Religion is worse than alluring drugs
For it reconcile man of himself to himself
So that he is none but right of self

-flattery is the poison that cripples all men

-Knowledge is painful
Ignorance is blissful
Wisdom is freedom

# BEST FRIEND

If I were the last to see you
And the first to leave you

If I were but steps upon you
Yet miles from you

If I were a friend to you
And an adversary for you

If I were the first to fight you
And the last to leave you

If I were the one to abandoned you
And the first to save you

If I were the first to argue with you
And the only one to agree with you

If I were your brother that walked the walk with you
And your ally that talked the talk for you

If I were the one that sticks closer than a brother to you
And the one that is brutally truthful for you

If I were the one that fought with you
And the one that fought for you

Then I'd be your best friend for life
And only death parts us

# Marriage

What is marriage if but for blissful fools
Declaring their troth with glittering jewels
Lured to walk under the yoke of iron rules
Clad with things of daily duels

Searching for something that refuses to be found
Even by the nose of the best of hounds
But lure me still till I am freely bound
And wrapped up thrills in a glowing gown

Hark hark oh night that hides the night
And leaves me but with little might
To see what fools declare alright
Dodging even the quest of daylight

Joined taxes are no thrill
And a mailbox with new fresh bills
Simply kills
And chills
A matrimony with but little frills

I be thrust through
Like the leaning flower from morning dew
Riveting heart of a loving you
Walking upon things that lovers do

How wonderful is a fool
To find another fool
To breathe the breath of the sweetest fool
And walk hand in hand in the in things only fit for a fool

Launch pass by brokenness
And help me reach my very best
Heal me of failed tests
Till I know how I am bless

Oh blissful fool am I
Dorn with jewels that money can't buy
And though I sometimes weep and cry
And want to throw my hands up and yell to this relationship goodbye

It be the glue that binds the broken pieces of me
The marred pieces secret pieces that others can't see
The eternal covenant between us three
God, my mate and me

# STAR OF NIGHT

Oh star that races across the velvety sky
Racing from nowhere to nowhere
Too wonderful for me to understand
Flying from the hymnals of yesterday
Into the masks of today
Blasting the skirts of eternity

And though I stare endlessly
Your sparkle vanish
Did you reach your destiny
Or did you grace too far for my eye to see

Every night I look up to see what I can see
Hoping to find another star
to light up the sky for me
and save me from my lonely nights
that others can't see

# DEAR GOD

DEAR GOD
GIVE ME THE WISDON TO LAY DOWN MY SWORD
WHEN THE BATTLE IS OVER
GIVE ME COURAGE TO STAND STILL
AFTER I HAVE FOUGHT A GOOD FIGHT
GIVE ME PEACE OF MIND
WHEN THE END IS NOT WHAT I SOUGHT
GIVE ME STRENGTH TO GO FORWARD
WHEN MY SOUL WANTS TO QUIT
AND TEACH ME THE DIFFERENCE BETWEEN
REAL VICTORY AND REAL DEFEAT

# COME FLY WITH ME

Come fly with me beyond the rocky shores
Of troubled waves and hollowed bays
Where turbulent wars find us no more
There we will bathe ourselves amongst peaceful caves

Come fly with me and ride upon the clouds of our blue sky
And rest upon the color filled never ending rainbow
Oh let your wings brave the sky
Where the holy cleansing winds from the east blow

Come fly with me in the sky so blue
Filled with imagination and no hesitation
Of too wonderful things of me and you
Thrust in dreams hued by no reservation

Come fly with me past our emotions
While still filled with gleeful emotions
Overcome by joyous notions
Where the sun and the clouds dance joyful commotions

Come fly with me where time stops
And days race
For stars that drop
And rest upon your face

Come fly with me
And then you will see
Wonder filled endless living for you and me

# HERO

You are a hero if you assume your responsibilities without badger
And you're not waiting for Mr. Charlie's Welfare to give your babies milk and clothes.

You are a hero if you go to work every day and receive unfair wages, but take your little wages and stretch it to cover those depending on you.

You are a hero if you chastise your children to groom them to be productive citizens and leaders of tomorrow.

You are a hero if you break away from your old friends, amidst regret and hurt, for you know that they're not good for you and where you're trying to go.

You are a hero if you keep your head on straight when everybody else is losing theirs and looking at you and wondering how you keep yours.

You are a hero if you refuse to stop dreaming, and force those that are connected to you to dream too.

You are a hero if you don't live in the past, but yet remember the past, and live in today, and prescribe tomorrow with availing hope, though it be challenging.

You are a hero if you stay with one woman or one man faithfully, and fight the temptation of outside love affairs that injure and kill blissful relationships as though they never were.
You are a hero if when you give you expect nothing in return

You are a hero if you can take care of someone else's children like they were your own, and never mention that they are not yours.

You are a hero if you can walk away after your heart has been broken, and tears fill your eyes.

You are a hero if you own up to and take care of the outside children that you shamefully and sinfully had.

You are a hero if you refuse the label of hero, and shout with all your heart that it is what a man is to do.

We need more heroes
Our wives need a hero
Our daughters need a hero
Our sons need a hero

But heroes don't just happen
We have to nurture and raise a hero to be a hero

# BEST FRIENDS FOR LIFE

"Oh why are you marrying for Leroy?" Bo said with clinched fist waving in the air. "You can't take no gal fishing or hunting with us."

"Didn't plan on it Bo," said Leroy. "Pappy says that it's just time for us to get ourselves a wife."

"Shoot, not me," said Bo. "They ain't nothing but trouble… Nothing but trouble I say."

"Well," Leroy started to say,

"My uncle says the only thing a man gets when he marries is more bills and headaches." Bo stirred, trying adamantly to make his point. "Why, when you get married, she won't even help you pay the bills; it's all on you; and if she got a job, she'll quit cause you become her pay day… No, no-sir- ree, leave me out of the marry stuff."

"And you're going to die a lonely old fool; just like Mr. Big John did last year," said Leroy.

"But Big John was crazy… very crazy. Who would want him? That crazy old coot." Bo said, preaching as hard as he could to Leroy.

"Well, I ain't dying alone," said Leroy. "besides, somebody is going to use you anyhow, and you can't take the stuff with you when you dies."

"So when you plan on marrying her?" Bo asked.

"Saturday." Leroy whipped without changing any expression.

"Saturday!!" Bo shouted. "Why, that's two days away. Are you crazy?" Bo shouted to the top of his voice.

“Yep, don’t see no needs to put it off,” said Leroy.

Bo shuffled back and forth, stirring around among the fallen brown leaves lying upon the ground. He could not believe it; no, he refused to accept it. He was about to lose his best friend, his only friend to a woman.
He had seen it happen too many times before. A woman comes in and takes over, and separate the man and his friends. What would fishing and hunting be like without Leroy, he thought to himself.

A gentle breeze blew softly from the south, shaking the trees as it blew. Brown leaves fluttered and glided slowing onto the ground and nestled upon the other leaves that had already fallen from the same tree. The sun was easing behind the tall trees to take its nightly rest.

Bo’s head swirled, his blood raced in his veins, and breaths rose sharply in his chest. He just couldn’t bare it… Just couldn’t bare the thought of losing his best friend to a girl.

Leroy just sat there ignoring Bo while he struggled to finish loading his back sack.

Bo reached down among the dying brown leaves, and grabbed a fallen branch of the tree, and raised it high in the air, and then brought it down hard across the back of Leroy’s head.

Leroy slumped over quietly without even a struggle.
“See what you made me do! See how she done already come between us. I told you… I told you.” Bo shouted at Leroy lying still upon the ground while his eyes, never blinking, stared aimlessly off into the adjacent bush. “Darn… Darn… Darn!”

Blood slowly crept down Leroy’s head and onto his neck and eased down his back, settling in his shirt, saturating it with a red hue.

Bo bent over and grabbed Leroy under his arms and dragged him to one of the big pine trees and propped him up against it. He started to whimper to himself, but no tears came from his eyes.

Bo paced back and forth, talking to Leroy who just sat there with his arms flung to his sides, and his big brown eyes, unflinching, seemingly staring back at Bo.

"Don't look at me like that!" Bo hollered at Leroy's body, and pointed his fingers as he did. "It's your fault- All your fault. Why you want to go off and marry. She was happy just being your girlfriend, but no… no, you want to marry and end our friendship cause you know that's what was going to happen; didn't you. You were just going to have more bills, and I was going to have to help you pay them in the long run. Damn… Damn… Damn!"

Darkness began to creep up among them. Leroy never moved an inch as death took the last of him; he just sat there staring as death settled in upon his flesh, stilling every bit of life that it could. His body began to get cold and stiff.

Bo rubbed his hands together, trying to muster some heat as he blew his warm breath into his hands.

"I got to make a fire cause I ain't through talking to you yet. This time I got you where you'll just shut up and listen." Bo said, looking around trying to see some wood that he can make a fire with.

He gathered some small branches and a bunch of leaves, and then nestled them together and struck a few matches. Suddenly and smoothly, a spark grabbed the dry leaves and branches and began to slowly smoke. Bo bent over, as if worshipping, and blew softly into the smoke. He blew and blew until a little flame eased up and licked the dry leaves and pieces of wood. The more he blew, the bigger the flame became.

Bo went off and found some more wood for the fire, and scraped together some more leaves.

It was now completely dark. Crickets and other creatures of the night began to scream to make their presence known. Bats skirmished around the darken sky looking for food, while the moon sat lazily upon the velvety grey sky.

It was a pretty silky night; a night filled with hope, and tomorrow's dreams; a night that Leroy didn't get to see, even though he was there propped up against a pine tree as his boyhood friend argued at him.

Bo talked and talked all through the night to a very silent still Leroy that stared blankly back at him.

"I told you over and over that girls ain't nothing but trouble, but would you listen to me… Nuhhhh, you had to go off and propose to that heifer; not even considering me. What about our friendship… Huh?" Bo shouted over and over again at the now paling Leroy.

"Oh God, I'll be no good in prison… You had to help me in my fights here… Shoot, truth is, and you know it; you fought my fights for me." Bo continued to argue at Leroy as the early morning crept slowly upon them. "How am I going to explain this to daddy? You just got us in a hot mess; just a hot mess… I can't go to jail!! Would you say something Leroy? Leroy please help me figure this out. I can't go to prison. You know um not good at figuring things out."

All through the night until the morning dew began to glisten upon the blades of grass, Bo pleaded his case to Leroy. He needed Leroy to come to his rescue as he always did.

A few days later, just before the golden sun began to descend beyond the distant mountains, a search team stumbled upon Leroy and Bo propped up against an old oak tree. They were staring blankly off into the distant forest. Bo sat shoulder to shoulder with Leroy, best friends to the end-just as they were in life. Tear drops of dried blood rested upon Bo's cheeks, and tiny drops of congealed blood lay in the hollow of his ears and stood crusted upon his neck.

"My goodness, what happened to these boys?" One of the men from the search team questioned as he looked Leroy and Bo's bodies over. "Leroy's head done been bashed in, but I can't figure out what happen to Bo. Looks like he just started bleeding from his insides."

A young girl wept hard as she stared at the two young men propped up against the old oak tree dead.

"One of them was your friend?" One of the women in the search team asked the young girl."

"Yea… Yea… Leroy was my boyfriend." She replied.

"Darn, probably a been a good husband to you one day too." The lady said to the young girl. "Heard that yall were engaged."

"Nahhhhh. We talked the last time that I saw him, and we agreed that it would be many years before we ever even considered such a thing. I was just happy being called his girlfriend." She said between hard sobs.

"Well, where did everybody get this marriage idea from." The lady asked her, scratching her head.

"Leroy wanted to trick Bo into believing that we were marrying soon." The young girl said, desperately trying to compose herself while she spoke. "I guess he never got a chance to fool him."

# TALE DON'T TELL

At last at last
My soldiers refuse to fight except when they so desire
And that be not often
And even then it be half heartedly

My honor my honor
Oh but for honor
I drop my head and remember when they would readily fight for me
That I might stick my chest out and raise my head
And declare the mighty man I be

My shame cloaks my face
And rests upon my lamentable shoulders
While others look at me and wonder why
My soldiers no longer fight for me

But still I demand that they arise
And conquer the battle at hand
Or else we be but nimble use to be want to be soldiers
Reaching for our youth of yester years

I shout to them
I collar them
Awaken from this slothful curse
And fight the fight that you once fought

Let us fight the fight
Where women praise us
And men envy us
And little children come for us

We are bold at night
And creep at day
Let us fight the fight of our youth
Where we never tire but fill our breast with joy

Arise at last old soldier
Where yesterday's victories rest upon your shoulders
Of fighting in the bush and smooth laden shores
Where praise walk hand in hand with pride

My gallant soldiers
I call upon you
Let us fight together but one more time
To fight together one more time
Until we rest together upon heaven's peaceful shores

women will remember and praise our fights
And tattoo our names upon the tables of their hearts
And wish for other soldiers to fight like us
So arise my soldier let us charge and thrust the enemy through
Until we be but spent of breath and strength till morning dew

# JEHOVAH'S GOODNESS

First before the mountains and seas were ever formed
First before the rivers and canals were ever torn
First before there was an evening or a dawn
Long before the first man was ever born
By Jehovah's power all of heaven was adorn

He shaped me in His image just after He hung the velvety sky
And placed the moon and sun up on high
Then flung the stars to light up the night sky
So that I can look up and know that He is always nigh

He is good
He helps me to accomplish all that I should
Protects me from all that would
And strengthens me to do what I could

Oh Great Jehovah as fresh as the morning dew
Piercing souls through and through
With wonders not a few
Watching over me with His angelic crew

I worship Him because of His goodness
I honor Him because in me He put His very best
To help me past my daily test
And walk in His eternal rest

In the bible His words are quoted
Riddled with spirit and power loaded
In-spite of this earthly flesh I am coated
In His image I am noted

Oh when lessened is health
And no earthly chores are left
I shall take my last breath
And embrace what mortal men call death
And live eternally in Jehovah's goodness and spiritual wealth

# PROVERBS

LOVE WON'T ALLOW YOU TO WALK AWAY PAINLESS
STILL, SOMETIMES YOU MUST WALK AWAY
EVEN WITH TEARS IN YOUR EYES
YOU MUST FORCE YOURSELF TO WALK AWAY
EVEN WHEN EVERY FIBER IN YOU PLEADS TO STAY
IF YOU SETTLE FOR SECOND
THEN YOU WILL ALWAYS BE SECOND
IF YOU ALLOW YOURSELF TO BE MISTREATED
THEN YOU WILL ALWAYS BE MISTREATED

BE CAREFUL VERY CAREFUL
WHAT YOU SAY
FOR YOU CAN NEVER TAKE A WORD BACK
ONCE IT LEAVES YOUR LIPS

NEVER FORSAKE YOUR FAMILY FOR A LOVER
FOR LOVERS CAN BE TEMPORARY
BUT FAMILY IS FOREVER
YOUR CHILDREN WILL ALWAYS BE YOUR CHILDREN
NO MATTER WHAT
BUT YOUR LOVER CAN DIVORCE YOU
AND BECOME SOMEBODY'S ELSE'S LOVER

PEOPLE LOOK AT YOU THROUGH YOUR OWN EYES
THEY WILL ALWAYS SEE YOU AS YOU SEE YOURSELF

# FOOL HEARTED

Tis the fool that believes in love
To loved love for the sake of love
To run and leap for the broken heart
To be disappointed and daunted endlessly

For lovers only become more human with time
And need more time to become human
Where faults and frailties multiply
And blemish never comply
Nor ever die

Oh fool that race to gulp the poisonous nectar of love
Where many a fools lie restless now
Weeping while wishing
broken heart never mending too soon

Love be the drunken liquor for fools
That dreams the dream of love for loves sake
For love is truly fake
Filled with fools seeking the mystical love for lovers to take

Though he promise never to fall in love again
But still
The fool won't fail to love quickly again
Knowing full well that love will soon break his heart swiftly again

# YOU

I saw the real you today
The real you that you had hid from me
Or the you that I refused to allow myself to see
The you that love feigned me to see
The you that dislodged your beauty so completely

I see you now so clearly
How were you able to hide from me
The true you so easily
Now I fret far too late of things of you I do see
Challenging me endlessly
Of what and who I should be

I can't take back what the false you stole from me
While in love with what you showed to me
Promising the lie of lie of what you could be
Making me to see what I wanted to see
Now I see the you I don't want to see
Marred torn and erupting so easily
Now I make my bed seeking to be free
From the real you that you hid from me

# GIFT OF LOVE

It is the gift that keeps on giving
And is not based upon reciprocation
It enhances the life of the living
And denies itself for the one it loves without reservation

THE GIFT OF LOVE
Oh that I might hide myself in burrows of yesterday
And blossom in the hope of a gleaming tomorrow
Where dreams and passions do lie and play
Desperately fleeing my wounding sorrow

THE GIFT OF LOVE
My heart my heart betrays me
While the whole of me yields of fairytales
Of things I blindly hope to see
And forge down dreams where others already fail

THE GIFT OF LOVE
Where a kiss be more than a kiss
And a touch be as a blame of eternal fire
Every lingering parted second be intensely missed
Feelings be more than feelings for hire or feelings that tire

THE GIFT OF LOVE
I breathe the breath of you
Never understanding the whole of me without the whole of you
Let us flee to do that for which only lovers do
And build loving dreams for dreaming lovers too

THE GIFT OF LOVE
Oh pierce me through
And saturate my heart
With endless thoughts of you
Every day is a forever start

THE GIFT OF LOVE
Oh love do hide me from me
That I may not forge down old paths and kill new dawns
Afford me to see the best of me
To see the best of you before these new feelings I do pawn

THE GIFT OF LOVE
Laughter and jubilee be my gift
And tears and sorrows I'll not flee
For to live and to love comes so swift
While the gift of love continuously renews me
To be the me that God created only in me

# PROVERBS

-To the world you can be a hero
But to your family and those closes to you
You will never be more than mere human

-You are superman to her until you get married

-When you become common
You lose your respect

-It is a fight to keep your wife from becoming your mother

-Those closes to you will never see the value of your worth until you are gone

-You can never teach a whore to be a lady
Or a dog to be a gentleman

# CHOOSE GOOD COMPANY

IF YOU WANT TO KNOW WHO YOU REALLY ARE? NOTE THE COMEPANY THAT YOU KEEP-THE PEOPLE THAT YOU CALL YOUR FRIENDS; THEY SPEAK VOLUME OF WHO YOU ARE. SPARROWS ONLY FLY WITH SPARROWS; PIGEONS ONLY FLY WITH PIGEONS; HAWKS ONLY FLY WITH HAWKS; BUSYBODIES ONLY HANG WITH BUSYBODIES; DREAMERS ONLY HANG WITH DREAMERS. SOMETIMES, TO BETTER YOURSELF AND MOVE HIGHER, YOU HAVE GOT TO CHOOSE NEW FRIENDS!!

# MISSING YOU

Sometimes the most difficult thing to do is to move on
To turn lose the wonder of the pass
And say goodbye to a loved one forever
To accept that you shall never see their face or hear them again

I journey in the privacy of my on thoughts
Shielded by secrecy
And making it just one day at a time
Feigning empty precepts and soiled joy

The daily battle is fighting depression
Through pretended strength
Even when your strength is nearly gone and depleted
It be a fight to even fight to fight

Rudely awakened by the grim reality that nobody really cares
Everybody lust for that piece of you that they can use
To further their own cause for comfort and security
They be blind
Walking in darkness during daylight
They be blind mouse forever searching for cheese

But I must fight on in-spite of my pain
My grandbaby's eyes pleads me to
Mama's silent voice shouts to me of things she taught me
Life is bigger than me
So sometimes we must choose to be the lamb of sacrifice
And allow others to use us
Even while we are yet bleeding and hurting

We must take our tears and sometimes wash their face
Take our things and stuff and give them hope
Even when they believe that they are using you
Or even when you know that you are being used
Be good for goodness sake
For that is how mama raised me

But still
The pain wrestles me daily
And often times win
But still I fight on because I know that's what you would have me do

I miss you
I miss you
I miss you

# VOID OF LIFE

YOU CANNOT DEVELOP GOOD RELATIONSHIPS
IN THE GRAVEYARD
AND A GOOD RELATIONSHIP WILL NOT CONTINUE
BEYOND THE GRAVE

# PROVERBS

THE UNIVERSE WILL BRING TO YOU
WHATEVER YOU BELIEVE WITH PASSION

AMONGST MEN
OPPOSITES DO NOT ATTRACK
YOU ATTRACK THAT WHICH IS MOST LIKE YOU
IF YOU DESIRE TO ATTRACK BETTER PEOPLE
YOU MUST BECOME A BETTER PERSON

YOU CAN NEVER TURN A SWINE INTO A GENTLEMAN
AND YOU CAN NEVER TURN A GOAT INTO A LADY
IF YOU TRY
YOU WILL ONLY HAVE A DRESSED UP HOG
AND A HARD HEADED WOMAN

IF YOU NEVER KNOW WHOSE YOU ARE
YOU WILL NEVER KNOW WHO YOU ARE
AND IF YOU DON'T KNOW WHO YOU ARE
YOU CAN NEVER WALK IN TRUE GREATNESS

YOU WILL NEVER STUMBLE INTO GREATNESS
TRUE GREATNESS REQUIRES
PLANNING AND GREAT EFFORT

# HOTEL OF LIFE

Life is like a great hotel
No one comes to stay forever
And everybody in there has baggage
Nobody can stay for very long
Everybody has a check out time

All kinds of people are in the hotel
And all are there for various reasons
It is home only for a little while
You never truly get to know your neighbors

At the end of the day you pay for everything
And when you leave somebody else will have your room
And sleep in your bed

# CHEATING ADULTERER

Hopelessly burden down with things that be so quickly fading
Upon packs and packs of troubles heavy laden
With man beast and even maiden
Life of life is simple raiding

Oh heart of hearts hoping to believe in somebody
But trusting to trust nobody

For all are but wretched liars
In search of helpless suppliers
Carrying a feign loving heart that be for hire
Whisking out upon the wind emotional fliers
To attract other hopeless liars

The thrust of pain is knowing they think you are but a fool
Just something for them to use like a handy tool
But I pity the using fool
For there is a golden rule

You reap what you sow
Even when you think that nobody know
Your deeds will surely come back to grow
And usually more than you are able to tow
For when they return they have to increased to grow

# PROVERBS

IF YOU STUMBLE INTO GREATNESS
YOU SHALL SOON BE A GREAT FOOL

IT IS HARD TO CONVINCE OTHERS
THAT YOU ARE GODLY
WHEN YOU ARE DRESSED worldly

YOUR WORDS WISPER
BUT YOUR ACTIONS SCREAMS ALOUD

A WOMAN IS MOST LIKE HER MOTHER
A MAN IS MOST LIKE HIS FATHER
IF YOU DESIRE TO KNOW BEFORE CHOOSING A MATE
SEEK TO KNOW THE CHARACTER OF THE MOTHER
AND THE CHARACTER OF THE FATHER
FOR THEREIN LIES YOUR FUTURE
FOR THE FRUIT NEVER STRAYS FOR FROM THE TREE

HER DRESS SPEAKS VOLUME OF HER CHARACTER

SHE WEARS MAKEUP BECAUSE SHE IS MADE UP
THE REAL WOMAN IS BENEATH

# THE OTHER WAY

They taught me to hate myself and to be materialistic
And to immolate them and every so often go ballistic
Because this life they serve me and expect me to live is not realistic
Always taking my gold my silver and giving me pretty worthless metallic

Teaching me to be blind but telling me I see
For from a youth they mold and shape me into what I should be
And what I should flee
They sell even slavery to me
For to them I am merely a commodity

I soon find that freedom is not free
Especially not for me
Born black and taken from the other side of the sea
Selling my soul for the highest fee
And discouraging my rebellion lest I hang from the highest tree

Now I awake and find a better way
And not listen to what they say
A better way to usher in a new day
I fight the fight come what may
For the new me is here to stay

My mind is elevated
My soul is motivated
Their bondage for me is annihilated
I be no longer isolated
to allow myself to be relegated

I choose the other way

# PROVERBS

IF SOMETHING DOESN'T FEEL RIGHT TO YOU
IT USUALLY ISN'T

IF SOMETHING SEEMS TOO GOOD TO BE TRUE
IT USUALLY IS

IF SOMEONE MAKES YOU FEEL
UNCOMFORTABLE INSIDE
EVEN THOUGH YOU CANNOT EXPLAIN IT
SEEK NOT AN ANSWER
STEP CAUTIOUSLY AWAY FROM THEM
YOUR HEART IS USUALLY RIGHT

ALWAYS RESIST THE HANDS THAT CHOKE YOU

IT IS THE FOOL THAT THINKS THAT SHE CAN DECEIVE
THE PROPHET WITH LIES

NEVER BITE THE HAND THAT FEEDS YOU
FOR THE NUTRIENTS WILL CEASE TO FLOW

# IN SEARCH OF MINE

I thrust my hands into the sandy banks of time
In search of that for which is truly mine
Far too long I've settled for that which only shine
Impatient and never waiting for that which define
That which is for me and only me one of a kind

IN SEARCH OF MINE

I shall never breathe my last breath
And wait around until nothings left
No I be no friends with old man death
Trying his best to steal my very self
And robbing me of the best of health
While chasing away my very wealth

IN SEARCH OF MINE

I force myself to go ahead
Down roads of uncertainty I am led
Where jewels of riches I will be fed
The gifts that come to me that I have said
Before I lay upon my eternal bed

IN SEARCH OF MINE

Oh hark oh hark to me oh hallowed heart
And lead me to a fresh new start
And put away this life of tart
Where the blessed of me shall never part
And the ignorance of ignorant shall be smart

IN SEARCH OF MINE

# PROVERBS

NEVER SETTLE TO BE A COPY
GOD MADE YOU AN ORIGNINAL

# Queen Bee

You can never make a Working Bee a Queen Bee
And you can never make a Queen Bee a Working Bee
For if you put the Queen Bee to work
She will still act like a Queen
And if you try to make a Working Bee a queen
It will still do the work

Accept people for who they are
They are best at being themselves
Than a good copy

# MEN OF VANITY

They come together within themselves
To reward themselves
With awards that they have made for themselves
For they are happy about themselves
Being the center of themselves
By themselves
For themselves

They praise themselves
For the work they have done for themselves
They are lost within themselves
And don't even realize that they are by themselves
Because they are in love with themselves

They talk to themselves
About themselves
Of how the world revolves around themselves
The most important one in their world is themselves

They teach themselves
Of doctrines they have made of themselves
For themselves
To honor themselves
Amongst themselves
For they be in love with themselves
And only themselves

# LOOK FOR ME

I contend with the world I live in
Of where I have been
A world filled with folly and sin
Of things beyond my mortal strength to mend

There is a now because there was a then
My present from which my past lend
They put me out because I was never in
Never given the chance to bath a win

I struggle and struggle to but mend
From the wounds they constantly send
Trying savagely my soul to rend
And make me forget from where I begin

Where am I in the end
With many a foes and but a friend
With few family and few kin
Standing alone wearing a fake grin

But I will look for me until the end
The real me that they tried to pin
And label and trap to only offend
In a society that rarely bend

One day they will look for me and remember when
And beg my forgiveness for way back then
For always trying to corrupt my mind with their Zen
And fill my soul with their sin

Look for me, I am just a screaming voice crying from within
About where I been
Wanting to find a listening ear of a friend
That I'll not offend
For hoping and praying to amend

Look for me, for my prayers I will constantly send
To be delivered from their sin
That they nurtured in me even before I begin

Look for me, in victory and triumph before the end
Look for me, never stop looking for me my friend
For the real me will come forth before the end
Look for me the real me from within

# SAY HELLO

Don't forget to say hello
To friend and even foe
Mama says everybody deserves a good hello
For never consider or even know
Just where they are about to go

Say hello
Even when you are feeling kind of low
Just say hello
And watch your joy within grow
Just because you said hello

From deep within your stomach bellow
A good hearty hello
Even after you have been dealt a hard blow
From someone you hardly know
Just say hello

The first sign to the other fellow
That you are someone that they should know
Is when you give a good hello
To someone you don't yet know
And you not give it just for show

When you can say hello
To your friend and your foe
Then you have mastered your feelings and become a pro
Just by saying hello
So never forget to say hello… Hello

# I AM AN AMERICAN

They say that I am an American
But they don't treat me like I am an American
I was born in America
But the constitution wasn't written for me
Or people like me

I am too dark you see
To be part of the brave and the free
I am the American they wish to hide
The America they don't pride
The America where my slave bearing fathers cried

I built their roads
Their fields I hoed
And from sun up till sun down I carried their load
While their clothes I sowed
Forever traveling down that lonely road
Of hoping to be an American before sold

I want to be an American
Even a black American
Or yellow American
Or brown American
Just an American

Where I can be a part of the revolution
And help strengthen the American constitution
I need not promised restitution
But free me from unfairly imprisoned institution

I am an American through and through
I didn't just appear here like the morning dew
But I was born and raised here by somebody they knew

Somebody they long ago slew
With their club bearing noose hanging crew

I fought on both sides of the civil war
Not really understanding what I was fighting for
I had to push slavery ajar
Never to accept it even from afar
I am an American the proof is in my deep riddled scar

Oh I am proud of red white and blue
Though not so proud of some of the things that we do
Still I am an American through and through
Even when I am discriminated because of my black skin's hue
In my heart I'll not let hatred brew
Because I am an American, that's what we do

I am an American through and through
Red white and blue
Many flee other nations to come here too
But they are not Americans through and through
1776 we started anew
And 1866 they grafted me in too
Now I am an American just like you

So I vote
And the ballad I tote
Because in America opinions float
And surround the White House like a moat

I am an American recognize me
And allow me to be
The American I long for you to see
An American that was born free
To help this country become as great as it can be

I am an American…

# CAUGHT UP

They say they left me behind
So that they can help me get caught up
But I wouldn't have to be caught up
If they didn't leave me behind

Just leave me alone
And don't try to fix me
Cause my problem is not me
My problem is you trying to fix me

Because you look behind to see me
Doesn't mean that I am behind you
It just means that I am watching you
Because of what you are constantly doing to me

I am left behind
Because I am caught up
And I am caught up
Because I was left behind

# DREAMER

I be dreaming but unbelieving
My nightmares are during my days
I am asleep but wide awake

Thoughts of yesterday torments me
While thoughts of tomorrow forsakes me
And thoughts of today imprisons me

Oh wretch that neither sleeps nor wakes
But dwell somewhere between
Day and night and eve of sight

# INTO THE DARKNESS

I close my eyes and I am connected to the rest of me
They fooled me to believe that what I see is actually real
When what I do see is what I have manifested for me to see
I was taught of the light
Deceived by the light
For the whole of me is in the darkness that you cannot see

The mass of darkness expands my soul
And connects me to the whole of the expanding universe
The whole universe expands
Thus I expand
For I am but part of the whole

The light shelters me from the darkness
Shelters me from the real authentic me
The largest part of me
The dark
But the little light taught me to be afraid of the dark

I am a prince born out of darkness
And imprisoned by light
And fooled to believe that existence is only what I see
But unbeknown to me
I created what I see
Therefore I am a part of the master of me

I close my eyes
And I can't see
But I do see
The best of me
Connected to the dark
The rest of me
With the rest of me

The dark swallows up the whole world
While the light regurgitates parts of it back
And fool me to think that the regurgitated parts is all there is
But I
Formed from darkness
Created the light

Out of the darkness
I created the light
To see what is not there
So that I can purpose the whole of darkness
And fool myself in the light

I am created from all that is
And all that ever will be
I am the last of the first
And the first of the last
I have always been
So then I will always be

Don't try and explain me
For you cannot explain what you cannot see
And don't be fooled by the light
For it only unveils what you choose to see

# SANTA IN MY NEIGHBORHOOD

I lay upon my bed swallowed up in covers
Staring out the darken window with ice everywhere
Because we have no chimney
I wait for a white man in a red suit to crawl through my window
The white man they call Santa Clause

Truly I don't expect him really
For how is he going to get passed the muggers and robbers
In my neighborhood
How is he going to get pass the fights and dealers
With all of those presents strolled over his shoulder

How is Santa going to get to a poor boy like me
Tucked away under the burden of raggedy covers
Shielding me from the killing cold
Cold that refuse to leave our little shack
Tucked away at the end of the street
Of the mean streets of my Hood

I hope they don't bother Santa
Cause he missed my house last year
Mama wept on Christmas morning cause Santa missed us
But not this year
I fight to stay awake so I can help Santa through my window
So mama won't cry this Christmas
For Santa and me

# WISH THAT I COULD BE MASTER FOR A DAY

Oh that I might be master for a day
I would not worry about what others say
For I would be master of all that day

In the heat of the day lying under a mulberry tree
Daydreaming of what a great master I would be
Over the other slaves that is not so free
I would let Mr. Charlie experience how hard slavery can be
Breaking your back day after day with no fee
So he would feel what it is like always desiring to be free

I won't work my slaves from can see to can't see
I would give them time to spend just with me
My slaves won't always be looking for a chance to be free
Or an opportunity to flee
They will be happy serving only me

If I was master for a day
I would make my slaves feel happy and gay
And give them off all that day
And render to them rest and warranted back pay
To show them that God hears them when they pray

Oh here comes master beaming
My slaves would say gleaming
While on their hoes leaning
And some of them in my house cleaning
I would tell one to do this and another to do that
And even have one to just carry my hat
I would stand with the other masters and chat
While my black skin aggravates them like a pestering nat
And smile at them like the cat that just ate the last rat

Oh here comes Mr. Charlie my way
He must have seen me under this tree napping today
And dreaming about being master for a day

I didn't free any of my slaves while I dream
I would just be another master of a different color it seam
That didn't even think to free my fellow slaves even in my dream

Master in any color is not good
Because he will never do right by his fellow man as he should

# PROVERBS

-MARRIAGE IS A SAFE HEAVEN FOR LAZY WOMEN

-A LAZY WOMAN WILL SOON BE SINGLE

-YOU CAN NEVER TRUST ONE THAT IS FILLED WITH LIES
FOR HIS LIPS WILL ONLY ISSUE WHAT YOU WANT TO HEAR

-VENOM RESTS UNDER A FOOL'S TONGUE

-NOTHING IS MORE TREASURED THAN SENSE THAT YOU PAID
A HIGH PRICE TO GAIN-BOUGHT SENSE

-THE FOOL SLEEPS SOUNDLY WHILE YOU WORRY ALL NIGHT

-YOU CAN NEVER MAKE A WHORE A LADY, NOR A LADY A WHORE

-THE BREAKING OF A NEW DAY ALWAYS EASES IN

-WISDOM WILL NEVER REST UPON THE LIPS OF A FOOL

# LOST

Every day I lose a little more of me
I see me disappearing in the night and vanishing during the day
I see a stranger staring back at me in the mirror
With wretched eyes and drying tears

Love pierced me through and hid in the grave
And placed a gulf that I cannot cross
Though I would if I could
So my heart be empty and faint
For part of me lay cold and still giving earth worms fill

But I forge ahead
For I am the sunshine of a few flowers
That glean towards me to blossom still
Giving others light while I fight through darkness that kill

I go on
Sometimes almost empty but I go on
Blinded and hurting but I go on
Used and abused by simple fools but I go on
I go on being the light to guild others path

I franticly search myself as best I could
As a careful policeman would
Reaching for the best of me that got lost in the worst of me
That even nature had hid deep in my eighborhood

Oh lonesome day oh fretful night
Flee me still and restore my might
That I might bolster again the passion to fight
And grasp a soul that is full of sight
Where earthen vessels scream of their right

Broken but I will find my way
Bleeding but I will find my way
Wounded but I will find my way
Weary but I will find my way

Because God left a light for the lost to follow
To find their way through pain and sorrow
For hope love and faith rest in my ability to borrow
A little bit of my dreams from tomorrow

# PROVERB

GOD LIVES IN THE SILENCE OF EACH MOMENT
HE DWELLS IN THE SOLITUDE OF
RECKONING ATTITUDES
HUSH, AND YOU WILL HEAR HIM
CLOSE YOUR EYES, AND YOU WILL SEE HIM
GRASP YOUR BREATHS, AND YOU WILL FEEL HIM
LISTEN… LISTEN TO THE SILENCE,
AND YOU WILL HEAR GOD
Whisper in your ears

I AM A PROPHET

SOME THINGS GOD REVEALS TO ME

I DON'T WANT TO KNOW

OTHER THINGS I KNOW

THAT I WISH THAT I DIDN'T KNOW

NONE THE LESS I AM STILL A PROPHET

GIVEN THE GIFT TO SEE AND TO KNOW

THAT WHICH IS UNSEEN AND UNKNOW

# GOD CREATED CHURCH

It is but God's hospital
Filled with the broken the bruised and the belittled
People that life has caused to be far too brittle
Like a collection of different vegetables boiling in life's kettle
Almost done but still needs The Master seasoning a little

People that know everything people that know nothing come for relief
Knowing that life is but a breath and far too brief
Praying that God will change their toxic death reeling belief
Before they lie beneath some pretty but loathsome reef
While others weep for them filled with grief

Oh but it is God's church
Where many a souls will end their search
And release the world that had become their crutch
Trying to gain worthless wealth and far too much

Where the dead meets the dying
And liars quit lying
Here the Holy Spirit be flying
While the sinners turn to saint while crying

God's church where man become clean through and through
From the evil deeds that he do
And become a part of the earthly angelic crew
Trying to save others who haven't got a clue

# Time

Tick tock
Hickory clock
That ramps and rage upon my block
And causes father time to knock
Of fleeting youth he desperately mock
Keeping me in a state of shock
Killing my every peer with whom I flock
While emptying my family's neighborhood block
Of failed successes that have been locked

Tick tock
Oh bewitched clock
That cast a spell upon my flock
And still my youth so quickly I drop

Tick tock
Now I run with the clock
Knowing full well that time is a mock

So watch not the clock
Cause it is locked
From future and past it rest on the dreary timeless dock

# The light in me

God put a light in me
So deep that you cannot see
But the universe can see
His light in me
Shining forth for the very stars to see

**PATIENCE**

**IS THE ICING OF VENEGANCE**

# BRUISING HEART

Oh here I go again
Carrying a bosom filled with lingering pain

Another time I wretchedly slip
From an unwanted withering relationship
Where joy and laughter have been stripped
And broken vows and unholy thoughts caress my lips

Oh here I go again having to explain my failures to the failures
While I seek again a rightly cure
From thoughts and things that's not so pure
And pray and pray for strength to endure
Till unfeigned love I can procure

Oh that my heart wouldn't be so fragile
And my emotions so agile
That love would come so gradual
To put an end to this unholy hassle
From day to night I wrestle

Let this heart of mind be mended
And let another be befriended
So my heart of hearts will no longer be offended
By some thoughtless one who hasn't strength to mend it

# CONTRARY PEOPLE

If I should live a thousand years
I shall never understand the least of man's tears
Or his many fretful fears
Of losing the things he holds so dear

They are angered about things that doesn't matter
And spend all their time worshipping things that they can gather
They chatter and chatter
About things and people that makes them sadder

Oh how miserable they must be
Blind of the things that they should see
The things that would make their souls so free
And their bodies of things so glee

They worship things and use people
And hope to hide their ugly ways under a church steeple
Trying their very best to allude the grim reaper
While their unholy lips deem them cheaper

They walk about like opened graves
Looking to find busybody slaves
Whose negative opinion they willingly gave
Making some fool of fools misbehave

Contrary people avoid them at all cost
For they will cause your soul to be lost
And your integrity to be tossed

# PROVERBS

-ALL LIFE IS BUILT UPON PRECIOUS MOMENTS
THUS, ONE MUST SEIGE THE MOMENT, FOR THEREIN LIES THE GIFT OF LIFE.

-TO SUCCEED, EVERY MAN MUST RIDE THE WAVE OF OPPORTUNITY

-IT IS THE POET THAT AWAKENS MAN'S CONSCIOUSNESS

-WHEN ONE LOOKS IN THE MIRROR ONE SHOULD SEE MORE THAN MERELY ONES REFLESHION. ONE SHOULD SEE THE IMAGE OF GOD LOOKING BACK AT THEM WITH ENDLESS POSSIBILITIES AND HOPE

-A SHEEP CAN BE NOTHING MORE THAN A SHEEP, BUT A WOLF CAN OFTEN DIGUISE AS A SHEEP

# OUR OLD SHACK

I am a man now,
But I often wish that I could go back to the old shack
Where I grew up in
The little shack where we shared rooms and shared beds
We were poor but didn't know it until we were grown
Hand me down clothes and hand me down shoes were our custom
And though we had little
We had much undoubted love
With our bellies full of whatever mama could gather
We always shared a good heaping of laughter

I miss those days when church folk were really church folk
That came to our shack making us uncomfortable with the bible
Our little shack was the gathering place for family and friends
We even had our little fights sometimes
But mama always forced us to makeup

Yes I miss our little shack
Where winters brutally attacked our shack
But mama stayed it with a crackling fire place
And warm quilts that were so heavy

And even though we had a big family in our little shack
No one went without
I miss our little old shack that simmered with love
Where the old guided the young
And the young obeyed and respected the aged
Our little shack where stories were told
And families were held together
With nothing but the cords of love

Now my little old shack stands empty
With weeds and vines growing up around it
And dust and time has over shadowed it
But I still remember the wonderful nurturing times in our old shack
Now I carry our little shack around in my heart
And share the principles that I learned in our little old shack
Would that everybody grew up in a little old shack
The world would be a better place
If everybody had a little old shack to remember

# A TALK WITH MAMA

This morning I walk through the cemetery talking to the dirt
Carrying in my bosom more than my share of hurt
I moan to relatives and old loves that won't even flirt
Silence unholy silence without even a prayer to assert

I bellow and bellow mama it's me
Eyes so full of tears I can't even see
But she won't even answer me
Like she use to so easily

Troubles just won't leave me alone
Fake and hypocritical souls even in my home
A host of feign love I have been shown
I be pierced through right down to my bone

Mama oh mama don't you hear my cry
Amidst this cold cemetery where others lie
Let me not die before I die
And have a little heaven on earth instead of in the sky

I be the living amongst the dead
With saving Holy Scriptures resting in my head
The ones mama sat me down and read
Every darken scary night before I went to bed

Now I hear mama whisper softly from the grave
Son you must live the life that God gave
It may be filled with bumps and storms but it is better than the grave
And always remember that Jesus still saves

Mama whispers the grave yard is not a place that I should be walking in
For the time will soon come when they shall carry me in
But until then
I should live for something to defend

Now I turn and leave mama's grave
Still I hear mama whispering to me to be brave
As I journey down life's road that's already paved
With many blessing that God has already gave

# FRIENDS AND ENEMIES

NEVER FORGET YOUR FRIENDS
AND
NEVER FORGET YOUR NENEMIES
FOR IF THEY ARE TRUE
THEY WILL NEVER FORGET YOU

# I AM BLACK

They say that I am black
Now everybody wants to fight for me
Fight with me
And make things right for me

What
Did they just realized I am black
Have they not seen my struggles
That did not start today or yesterday

I am black today
But I was black yesterday
And the day before
I have always been black

But all you saw was a strong back
That didn't deserve any rights
To be upheld in the streets or on the farm
You approached me with only a day's work
And no pay

But I made it through
In spite of you
In spite of the sun bathing me
In spite of your lashing whip and harsh tongue
I made it through

You taught me to despise my black skin
Despise my brown eyes
Despise my nappy hair
And anybody that looked like me

I have been brain washed to look like you
So I bleached my skin
Colored my eyes
And fried my hair to be straight like yours
But still you won't recognize me as equal

I am still black
And daily you remind me
That there is a gulf between you and me
A gulf that I tried desperately not to see

You say I am part of the constitution
Well why then did you have to amend me in
And why then did even some of the signees have slaves like me
No your constitution was written by you for you

I am still black
And I have learned to love my velvety black skin
That the sun rested upon
And though many of my brothers and sisters fry their hair
I love my nappy curls that rest upon my head

I am black
And I shall always be black
I am the best of my Fathers children
I shall remain black
Cause it flows deeper than just the color of my skin

Black is even in the blood that runs through my veins
Right down to the genes that cluster in me
So thought I am black
I come in all shades of color
Red brown caramel dark
But I am still black
Like God created me to be

# DEATH

Why do you keep following me
Chasing me
Ravaging me
Tormenting me

You are always stealing from me
Stole my father and my mother
And my siblings and other relatives too
Now you are staring at me
And reminding me that someday you shall come for me too

But I be not afraid
For I shall live until I die
I refuse to die before I die

I simply refuse to live in fear of you
So come let us walk down the road together
I shall be conscious of you
Knowing full well that you follow me

Come now oh life of the living
Let me taste every drop of the sweet nectar of the living
And even the bitter shall be made sweet
Until I lay upon my eternal bed to rest
And embrace the one that have been following me all of life

I fight the fight
And care the care
And rest the rest
Until all of me is spent upon life
When he that has followed me all of life
Shall come for me
I shall be but spent
And ready to walk down new paths upon the other side

# PROVERBS

BE CAREFUL WHAT YOU SAY
FOR WORDS CANNOT BE RETRACTED
AND SAYING I AM SORRY DOES NOT ERASE HURT

NEVER GET VALUE AND WORTH MIXED UP
VALUE IS THE COST
WORTH IS IN THE HEART

APPRECIATE THE PRESENT
FOR ONCE IT LEAVES
YOU CAN NEVER GET IT BACK
IT SOON BECOMES THE SPOILS OF THE PAST
FOR WHICH YOU CAN NEVER GET BACK

MAKE THE MOST OF WHERE YOU ARE RIGHT NOW
FOR ALL OF LIFE IS FILLED WITH
BUT FLEETING MOMENTS
THAT SHALL SOON PASS

LOST LOVE CAN NEVER BE REKINDLED

IF YOU WANT TO KNOW WHAT KIND
OF HOUSE WIFE SHE SHALL BE
NOTE HOW SHE KEEPS
HER BATH ROOM, HER CLOSET, AND HER BED ROOM

HE WILL NEVER TREAT HIS WIFE BETTER
THAN HE TREATED HIS MOTHER

# DAMNED FOOL

In love with even the thought of being in love
I am slain by even the gesture of love
My breaths are taken away by love
I convince myself that my reward is love

Love hides itself from me
So I am often confused by what I see
For I leaped blindly into something I thought was for me
But I find that Feign love is costly it is never so free

Oh wretch am I
Never having wings but wanting to fly
While watching other birds that fly so high
Wanting to flee things that make me cry

Over and over I tell myself that I will be fine
And I say but this time
But this time I say but next time
Then next time I hope for another time

Damned damned damned
Running to my shearers like a lamb
If I fail this time I'll be damned
My heart be crammed
Full of tears for the damned

But I learned this time
What to do next time
But that is what I said last time
Before this time

Damed damed damed am I
Wanting to fall in love again before I die
I search and search the never ending sky
To love again before I give up the ghost and die

# SECRET LOVE

My eyes eased across the room to you
I caught your gaze before you leaned to break free

I ponder had you felt what I felt
A ravaging salvage of love inside beckoning to be free

But look at me
Looking across the room at you

Wondering if you feel the way I do
But I can tell that you secretly do

But you must hide what you truly feel
For that is what we do

Flash a gentle smile
And hope upon hope that they will catch it

And ease a door open
A door that I may ease through

But I keep my pride in check
And hope that you'll not rest upon your pride

No please don't slay the moment
That I have secretly stolen just for us

But bath this once
In chance of romance
Ease me through
Before I die of hope of meeting you

Imagine the warm embrace
And the sweet nectar of a kiss

You walk away
And I wonder when will I see you again

But I live in hope
The heavenly host takes note of budding love

So I should wish for another chance
Of meeting your eyes across the room

And ease so boldly
To make a love so freely

Until then
I hope upon hope
That I shall see you again

# THE DECEIVED LIAR

ALL LIARS THINK THAT EVERYBODY IS A BLINDED FOOL
FOR THEY CONVINCE THEMSELVES OF THEIR OWN LIES
AND WALK UPON THE CLOUDS IN THE SKY
WHILE SHACKLED TO THE MOLDEN EARTH BENEATH

# YOUR SMILE

Oh pierce me through
With a glimmering smile just from you
And chase away all of my blues
With sweetest thoughts of you

Oh smile smile for me
Or smile smile at me
And forge my heart upon rivers rampant to be
And bellow my soul of ever so free

Your smile like a rose hanging upon a stem
That chase away my nights that is ever so dim
And days that is full of hidden grim
Let it sparkle upon me like a precious gem

Toss your smile at me and I shall catch it as a butterfly
And hold it upon my heart and keep it ever so nigh
Though your beauty forces me to be bashfully shy
Your smile slays me like a gentle baby's cry

I gaze at you while you gracefully walk away
But your smile lingers with me like a cool breeze upon an ocean's bay
And I ponder and ponder will I see you another day
And if so would I know just what to say

# Proverbs

YOU WILL NEVER CATCH A MAN
IF YOU TAKE AWAY THE HUNT
AND
YOU WILL NEVER KEEP A MAN
IF YOU CEASE TO BE THE SPOIL

IF YOU TALK TO A MAN LONG ENOUGH
HE CANNOT HELP BUT TELL YOU
THE TRUE INTENTIONS OF HIS HEART
FOR TRUTH CANNOT BE HIDDEN LONG

# NOTES

# NOTES

# NOTES

# NOTES

# NOTES

Printed in the United States
By Bookmasters